How to TELL TiME

A Step-by-Step Guide for Kids and Their Grown-Ups

by the editors of Klutz

A Note to Grown-Ups:

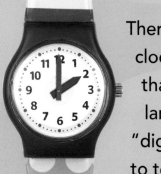

Welcome to the world's simplest set of directions for how to tell time. Unlocking the mysteries of time telling is a rite of passage for all kids. This book is designed to help you get them through it. Read the book together, set the watch together and practice telling time together. **Above all, have a good time!**

Meet Your Watch

There are two kinds of watches and clocks in the world. We call the kind that comes with this book the "regular" kind. The other kind is called "digital." This book will teach you how to tell time on the regular kind of watch.

regular

digital

YOUR left hand

YOUR right hand

There are two hands on the face of your watch. They're called "hands" even though they are just pointers.

The short hand is called the "hour" hand, and it moves the most slowly. The long hand is called the "minute" hand and it moves more quickly by "jumping" a little bit every time a minute passes.

the short hand
(the most important one)

the long hand
(the next most important one)

3

How to Get Your Watch Started

Step 1

Ask a grown-up what time it is. (By the time you finish this book, you can ask yourself what time it is. But for now, you need an adult.)

Step 2

Push in the little knob on the side of the watch. Keep holding it in until your grown-up says the watch shows the correct time. Let go of the knob — your watch is set!

How to Change the Battery

Your watch runs on a battery. It looks like this: After about half a year, the battery will wear out. You can buy replacement batteries at drugstores or jewelers.

Have an adult help you take the back off the watch. Pop out the old battery and slide in the new one. Then replace the back. You're back in business.

See battery use tips on inside back cover.

Watch out!

Stay out of the bathtub and the swimming pool with your watch. It definitely does not like water.

The Hour Hand

The short hand counts hours. It is the snail on your watch. **S L O W !** Looking at it, in fact, it doesn't seem to move at all. But it does. In a full day (from breakfast to breakfast) it goes around the watch twice.

Rule 1   The big rule in this book is to count hours first and count minutes second. (We'll tell you all about counting minutes in a couple of pages.) For now just remember to always, always, always count hours first.

Rule 2

To count hours, look at the numbers on the watch. The numbers stand for the hours.

 3:00

 9:00

So every time the hour hand points exactly at a number, it is exactly that hour. If it points exactly at the 3, it is exactly 3 o'clock. If it points exactly at the 9, it is exactly 9 o'clock.

So far so good.

Most of the time,
however, the hour
hand is not pointing
exactly at a number.
It's pointing between
the numbers.

That's OK.
Here's how to deal
with that.

If it's a little past
the 3, say, "It's
a little past 3."

If it's a lot past
3, say, "It's a lot
past 3." Or you
could say, "It's
almost 4." That
means the same
thing.

But what if it's right in the middle, right between the 3 and the 4? Then what? No problem. Just say, "It's half-past 3." That means the hour hand is halfway to the next hour.

That's pretty much it. If you like, you can stop reading right here since you have now learned about the most important hand on the watch — the short, hour one. Take a break. Put on your watch and go play for a while. See if anybody wants to know what time it is.

Hey, wait for me!

The Minute Hand

You're back. You must be curious about the other hand on your watch, the long one. It counts minutes.

Look around the edge of your watch. Each of those dots, black or red, stands for a minute. When the minute hand goes from one dot to the next, that means a minute has passed. If you watch the long hand carefully, you'll see it jump from one dot to the next, to the next.

There are 60 minutes in an hour (just like there are 60 noses right here).

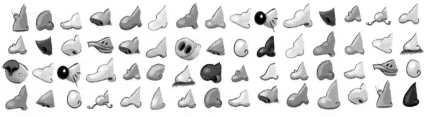

If you watched for a whole hour, you would see the minute hand go all the way around the watch, jumping from dot to dot to dot. But don't do it. Way too boring.

On your sixth birthday, you have lived 3,153,600 minutes. An adult can help you figure out exactly how many minutes old you are right now. And tonight. And tomorrow.

Stuff that takes about 1 hour:

eating 12 ice cream cones

two TV programs

big trip to the grocery store

Stuff that takes about 1 minute:

two TV commercials

getting dried after a bath

eating one chocolate chip cookie

Time to Tell the Exact Time

Let's say someone asks you what time it is. Your watch looks like this:

What time is it? Just like always, you look at the short hand first. It's pointing about halfway between the 2 and the 3. So you say, "It's about half-past 2."

But, maybe this person is picky. She wants to know exactly how many minutes it is past 2 o'clock. Now you're going to have to look at the minute hand and count the minutes.

Here's where Rule 3 comes in.

Rule 3

To count minutes, you look at the dots around the edge. The dots stand for minutes.

So on this watch start counting dots from the dot at the very top, right above the 12. Stop when you get to the dot that the long hand is pointing toward. How many did you count? (We count 27.) That's how many minutes it is past the hour, so say, "It's 2:27." (Oops, it took you a minute to read the watch. Now it's 2:28.)

A Shortcut

Maybe you noticed that some of the dots around the edge of the watch are red. We put those dots there for people who know how to count by 5s.

Start here.

Count these dots by 5s.

Every time you get to a red dot, that equals 5 minutes.
So you can count more quickly by counting red dots only
and saying "5. . .10. . .15. . . ," like that. Start at the top.
When you get to the first red dot from the top, that's "5."
Now go from there.

If the minute hand is not pointing
exactly at a red dot, you might
have to count a few black dots
right at the end to get the
exact number, but it's
still a lot quicker than
counting all the way
by 1s.

5, 10, 15, 20
25, 30, 35,
40, 45, 50

What Time Is It Exactly?

The short hand is pointing between the 5 and the 6. That means it is after 5 o'clock. How much after?

Starting at the top dot, count each dot all the way to the big hand. We got 18. What did you get?

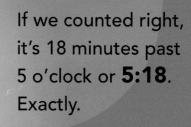

If we counted right, it's 18 minutes past 5 o'clock or **5:18**. Exactly.

The Only Rules in This Book

1. Count hours (with the short hand) first. Count minutes (with the long hand) second.

2. Look at the numbers to count hours.

3. Look at the dots to count minutes.

What about when the hands hide behind one another?

Sometimes when you look at your watch, it looks as if the short hand has disappeared. Don't be fooled. The hour hand has just hidden behind the minute hand for a minute.

Follow your normal rules: Even though you can't see all of it, you know where the short hand must be hiding. Look at the number the hour hand has passed, then count minutes up to the long hand. So this watch says it's 10:54.

Just a minute...

Although a minute is always the same, no matter what you are doing, it can seem like a very long time if you are waiting for someone to get out of the bathroom.

Hour after hour...

On the other hand, an entire hour goes by very quickly if you are reading your favorite book.

Day and Night

Don't worry, the hard part is over. There's just one last thing you need to know. Remember we said that in one full day, say, from breakfast to breakfast, the hour hand goes all the way around the watch face twice?

It goes around once for the morning hours, from midnight to noon, and around once for the afternoon hours, from noon back to midnight.

The regular kind of watch doesn't tell you whether it's 1 o'clock in the morning or 1 o'clock in the afternoon. You have to do that just by looking around you. Did you just eat lunch and are still in school? That means it's 1 o'clock in the afternoon.

Are you asleep? (Don't wake up to ask yourself.) That means it's 1 o'clock in the morning. Everybody else, even the picky people, will know that, too, when you tell them "It's 1 o'clock." Just so you know they know you know.

More Great
Chicken Socks™
Books

Make Your Own Twinkly Tiaras
Melty Beads
The Foam Book
Magnetic A to Z
Highlight This Book!
Pop Bead Critters
Amazing Lacing
Totally Tape
Rescue Trucks
How to Make Pompom Animals
Hand Art
Shadow Games
Utterly Elegant Tea Parties